Publish Today!

Publish Today!

A Helpful Guide
to
Book Publishing
for
Authors and Self Publishers

Celia Webb
and Mack H. Webb, Jr.

Pilinut Press, Inc.

Publish Today!
A Helpful Guide
to
Book Publishing
for
Authors and Self Publishers

The pilinut is the edible seed of the *Canarium ovatum* tree which is native to Southeast Asia. Tasting like sweet almonds, it is eaten for its health benefits including prevention of anemia and for nourishment of the brain and nervous system.

Library of Congress Control Number: 2009928220
Printed in Warrenton, Virginia

ISBN 978-0-9779576-7-5

Book and cover design by Celia Webb
Cover Art by Celia Webb

Pilinut Press, Inc.
www.pilinutpress.com

Table of Contents

Chapter 3: How to Work with a Subsidy Publisher

Chapter 4: Self Publishing

Chapter 1:

Introduction to Publishing

Getting Started

So you have decided to publish and/or illustrate a book. Great! You will find that there are a lot of rewards and benefits associated with publishing. You will also find that there is a fair amount of work involved.

Getting anything published can be a time consuming, bewildering, and disheartening experience if you have never published before, and sometimes, even if you have.

Publish Today! is a quick reference designed to demystify the writing, designing, publishing, and marketing processes with the goal of getting your product into the hands of the end consumers. Let's get started!

Overview of the Publishing Industry

Fifty years ago the publishing industry consisted of only a few large publishing houses. These houses were swamped with manuscripts, and often several years would pass before hopeful authors received word concerning their prized manuscripts. Some authors never received word. Reviews by the publishing companies were very difficult to come by. Without a review there can be no publishing contract and, therefore, no published book.

Today there are literally tens of thousands of mid-sized and smaller publishing houses. The smaller publishing houses emerged when technological advances made it possible to produce, market, and distribute a book at a relatively low manufacturing cost. What this means to you is there is a greater chance that your manuscript or book will get published. Additionally, other publishing options are now more available than ever before – subsidy- (vanity) and self-publishing. In **Publish Today!,** we will explore all of these options so you can determine what will work best for you. We will thoroughly explain subsidy- and self-publishing as these two options are the fastest methods of getting published.

The Bird's Eye View: According to Bowker's annual listing, *Books in Print*™, there are about 1.7 million books in print each year. Roughly 195,000 new titles emerge each year while other books are taken out of print status. The book industry is a 28 billion dollar a year business. The United States is the largest market for books (based on total sales), followed by Japan, Germany, the United Kingdom, France, Spain, South Korea, Brazil, Italy, and China.

The largest category-markets for books in order of total sales listed from highest to lowest are: Professional Books, Elementary-High School, College, Adult Trade Hardcover, Adult Trade Softcover, Mass Market Paperback, Children's Softcover, and Children's Hardcover.

The top five publishers (Random House, Simon & Schuster, Bantam Double Day, Time Warner, and Harper-Collins) control 60% of trade book sales. Bookstores account for 71% of trade books sold of which 33% are frontlist (new releases) and 67% are backlist books. Only one in ten books released by the top five publishers makes back the advance paid to the author. Among mid-size publishers, roughly 60% of all general trade titles may lose money.   Publishers rely on bestsellers to keep their companies solvent.

Since 1970, the number of small publishing ventures has ballooned from 3,000 to over 60,000. Eight to eleven thousand new publishers enter the book trade each year. The rapid growth resulted from four major changes: short-run printing technology; computer and desktop publishing programs; bookstore distribution opening up to the small publishers; and increased dissemination of knowledge cutting the learning curve for new publishers. Small publishers or self-publishers now publish 78% of all new books.

Small publishers and self-publishers often use printing companies which can produce very small print runs. The technology which enables this approach is called Print-On-Demand. The average book printed by a Print-on-Demand company sells between 75 and 200 copies, mostly to family and friends of the author. Only 3% of self-published books sell more than 1000 copies. Only 1% of self-published books sell more than 5000 copies.

Despite the interest in moving to digital means of transmitting knowledge, eBooks have been slow to take off. While the newspaper industry is suffering the effects of people moving to the internet to keep up to date, tangible books are still very much alive. Additionally, when consumers do switch to eBooks, publishing houses can accommodate the switch easily. The switch by customers to digital delivery is dramatically changing the world of newspaper publishing. While newspapers can switch to the internet, the advertising money available on the internet is miniscule compared to what is charged for a printed page. Newspapers rely on advertising dollars to meet operating expenses, book publishers do not.

Large and mid-size publishers give most books four months to prove they are marketable. If the books prove to be otherwise, the unsold books are pulled from the shelves and go through a process called "remaindering", which means they are sold for whatever the publisher can get for them to help cushion the loss. These are the books you can pick up for a song at grocery stores and bookstores. In order for a book to be successful, the author must participate in the marketing process.

Most authors are under the misconception that the publisher will promote the book. In fact, very little effort goes into promoting any book except for the "guaranteed best seller". Traditional publishers know that more than 90% of books will not pay back the advance paid to the author. They gamble on acquiring some best sellers to pay the bills. Other books may be developed to round out their catalogs, but are not really expected to make a return on their investment.

Publishers versus Printers: Publishers invest in book projects which they guide and develop from beginning to end. They take on the financial risks associated with producing a book. The process includes the acquisition of the rights for publication; editing, the book design, printing, marketing, the distribution, and customer fulfillment. They purchase blocks of ISBNs from the agency authorized

4

by the US government and assign a number to an individual book.

Printers manufacture books. They invest in the book's production at any phase and perform no editorial functions. They neither acquire nor assign ISBNs. They may provide shipping and some distribution functions on behalf of the publisher.

Some printing companies have become "subsidy" publishers. These companies blur the clear line that traditionally separated the functions of publishers and printers by offering some services which, in the past, were only offered by publishing companies. One of the services is providing an ISBN. These companies may also provide pay-for-service options for editing, book design, and some marketing. Most printing companies which have taken this approach advertise as "self-publishers". They are actually subsidy- (also called vanity) publishers meaning you pay them to print your book. They invest nothing in your book project.

How Bookstores Work: The book trade is unique in the retail world in terms of the expected trade discounts and the returns policies. Trade discounts are the percentages off the retail price at which the publisher sells the book to the distribution channel. The standard markup for retail items like clothing is 50%. The standard trade discount for books is 50 to 60%, but many books are offered at even greater discounts in the range of 70%. Some book selling channels like book clubs or promotional item sales expect an even bigger discount like 90%. You will see later in this book how the discount structure for some book markets drives printing decisions. (See Appendix D for an example.)

The other unique feature of selling through bookstores is the industry standard for returns. In most of the retail industry, there is either a "no return" or a "limited return" policy set by the manufacturer. If there is a return policy, it is usually no more than 90 days from time of purchase. The publishing industry standard is that books may be returned to the publisher from bookstores for any reason and in any condition for up to six months from the time of the store's acquisition.

For the publisher these two policies mean the production costs for their books must be tightly controlled. Any books sold to bookstores which do not sell may be returned. Money which was paid for a book in June may need to be refunded in December. It is one of the reasons why royalty payments lag significantly behind the initial date of sale. The sale is not really final until six months later.

Publishing Options

As little as ten years ago, publishing of their book was beyond the reach of most authors. However, times have changed. New technologies have been introduced which allow authors to publish and distribute a book worldwide. Today there are literally thousands of books being published each month. Authors have several options when they decide to publish their book.

The following sections explain the various options available in publishing, give information regarding access to resources, and provide tips on publishing.

Publishing can be thought of as a three part process: writing, producing, and marketing. An author who understands all these phases can help his book reach an interested audience. Most authors concentrate on writing the book. That is certainly the important part of the process. However, an author also needs to know that only through much effort on his part during the marketing phase will the book be sold in any appreciable number.

It takes many steps to take a book from a concept to a finished product. Different publishing options provide varying services to cover these steps. Traditional publishing can be thought of as the full-service option. The publisher takes responsibility for taking the book from the draft of the manuscript through all other steps to a completed product and may do some marketing for the book. Self-publishers must contract or perform themselves all of the steps to get a book to market.

Traditional Publishing: The traditional publishing method is for an author to submit a manuscript to a publishing company for consideration. If the publishing company selects the manuscript, the publishing company invests in the book by buying the rights, developing the book, printing and distributing it, and, perhaps, marketing it. Traditional publishing companies give a book about four months on the market to prove it can make money. If the book does not meet sales expectations, it is "remaindered" (meaning the remaining copies are sold for whatever the publisher can get).

Publishers have "publication programs" which define the types of books they specialize in publishing. They do this for production and marketing reasons. Finding a publisher for your cherished work can be easier if you make sure you submit your manuscript to interested publishers. The closer you can get to matching a publishing program, the better since the publisher has already developed a marketing plan for your type of book. A great way to do this is by perusing a book titled *Literary Market Place*™. Most libraries carry the two-volume annual publication in the library's reference section. If you do not see it on the shelves, ask the reference librarian for assistance.

Literary Market Place™ lists all publishing companies in the United States and Canada which accept unsolicited manuscripts. Contact information and descriptions of their publishing program are listed in several cross-referenced sections.

Literary Market Place™ also has a fee service available on-line at **http://www.literarymarketplace.com**.

Illustrations: Do not worry about finding an illustrator if you are concentrating on finding a publisher. Almost all publishers would rather take care of matching an illustrator to any project they undertake for primarily two reasons.

1. Publishers have to obtain the rights to anything they print and they have more room for negotiation if they contract directly with the illustrator.

2. Publishers typically have a group of illustrators they work with who they know will meet their timelines and publication requirements.

Publishers will want to make the book fit into their publishing program. Sometimes this is accomplished by the look and feel of the book which is determined, to a great degree, by the illustrations used.

How to Approach a Publisher: Before incurring the cost of mailing a manuscript, send a query letter to the publisher. This letter should be one page only and contain:

1. Your contact information

2. A brief description of the plot line (maybe a paragraph in length)

3. A description and size of the target audience and how you plan to reach them.

With this letter include a stamped self-addressed postcard. On it fill in the publisher's return address (so you know which publisher returned your card) and mark a line on which an interested editor can fill in her name so that you will be able to address your manuscript directly to her. The purpose of publishers is to sell books. In this query letter show yourself to be an author who is aware of, and willing to participate in, the kind of marketing that ensures successful sales.

You must market to the end customer, not bookstores. By the way, the term "end customer" is a marketing term used to differentiate the individual consumer who buys the book in order to read it from the retailers who buy the book in order to sell it. The way the publishing industry works is different than other forms of retail. When a bookstore buys a book, it can be returned, for any reason, up to 6 months from the time of purchase. So you want to have customers driving demand at the bookstores. The end customer, not the bookstore, must be convinced of the value of your book.

For an authors who is not a household name, the book must be "hand sold" (meaning a person recommends it to a buyer). Most bookstores do very little hand selling.

There are plenty of other ways to market books. You can find lots of ideas in *"1001 Ways to Market Your Book"* by John Kremer.

Understanding how to market a book will help you whether you are self-publishing or trying to publish through a traditional publisher.

Subsidy Publishing: Subsidy (also called vanity) publishing allows authors to pay for their books to be published. The subsidy company provides book design, printing, and distribution services.   For an additional payment, the company may also provide some marketing services.

Subsidy publishers do not advertise their companies by using the terms "subsidy" or "vanity" publishing. Instead, they most often advertise as "self publishers". Searching the Internet using the keyword "self publisher" will show the companies who offer these services. Some of the most well known of the subsidy publishers are:

www.AuthorHouse.com
www.iUniverse.com
www.Xlibris.com
www.CreateSpace.com
www.Lulu.com

Most professional reviewers will not review subsidy published books. This is partly because of the numbers of these books that get published (the top two subsidy publishers release about 1,000 books per month) and partly because the books tend to be poorly edited. They are just not as well put together as the books which have gone through the more rigorous process applied by a traditional publishing house.

Using a subsidy publishing company does, however, make sense for a number of situations including the following.

- A book which is the product of a classroom project

- Groups which want to do a fundraiser book for their organization (like a cookbook)

- An author who is recording a family history and wants the rest of the family to be able to buy copies

- An author who anticipates that sales will be limited to family and friends

Another strategy which could lead to success is for the author to use a subsidy publisher to produce a book which he then markets intensively to try to reach the "1,000 books sold" mark. Once he reaches that mark, he markets the book to publishers who have publishing programs which match his book.

Self Publishing: Self publishers set up their own publishing companies and handle all aspects of book development. This is a serious commitment on the part of the author. The company may grow to the point that it takes on other publishing projects. Some services (like printing) may be contracted out.

Self publishers write, edit, illustrate, design the interior and cover, print, distribute, market, and promote their books. They must acquire a block of ISBNs, file for copyright, obtain barcodes, and Publication Control Numbers. They retain full creative control over their work.

In contrast, once a traditional publisher has acquired a manuscript, they often re-work it to fit their market.

Sometimes this results in tremendous changes to the manuscript; the title may be different, the writing style altered, even plot points may be changed to fit the publisher's idea of what buyers will purchase. Some authors are loathe to give up their story to these types of changes. The contract you sign with a publisher can specify that the author retains creative control, but this is not a clause that most publishers include automatically.

Additionally, any traditional publisher may take up to two years or so before publishing the work. They may decide in the end, not to publish, and the author will have lost two years or so in which the book may have been released. And finally, to the traditional publisher, author compensation is a percentage of books sold after publishing costs have been subtracted typically between 8 and 10%. James Michener, a very famous author, who has sold millions of books, reportedly said he wished he had been paid one dollar for each book sold. He would have made more money!

Authors usually choose the route of self publishing because they can retain creative control, see their work published swiftly, and reap the rewards of doing so.

Quick Summary of Publishing Options

Traditional Publishing – you find a publisher who is willing to put up the money to fully develop the "property" (read book) and pay you via royalties and/or an advance.

Advantages:
- All production is handled by the publisher.
- You may get some marketing assistance from the publisher.
- Reviewers will review your books.

Disadvantages:
- Editorial control typically rests with the publisher, unless specifically addressed in the publishing contract.
- You may need to get a literary agent in order to be considered by a large publishing firm.
- You usually have four to six months to prove your book will sell. If it does not sell well, the book will be pulled off the shelves, and be "remaindered". The book will go out of print.
- You will be the primary source of marketing no matter which way you publish. It is smart to develop a marketing plan for yourself prior to any publishing commitment. The traditional publisher may help open some doors and may do some advertising for you, but unless you are a celebrity writer, you will not receive much marketing help. This seems really strange, we know, but that is the way the industry operates.

14

Self Publishing – you set up a company, buy ISBN's, and control all aspects of production and marketing.

Advantages:

- You have editorial control and can develop a property just the way you want (this could be fine or it could be a disaster depending on your understanding of the book market).
- You can develop your market over more time. You can keep your book in print and available for as long as you want.
- Your profit is largest per book sold.

Disadvantages:

- You must run a business with all the associated responsibilities and requirements.
- You must educate yourself on all the processes associated with the publishing industry and be willing to do all the things that are required to produce and market a book or hire someone to do them for you.
- Some reviewers may not review your books.
- You must provide front-money to produce the books and operate the business.

Subsidy (Vanity) Publishing – you pay a publisher to produce your book.

Advantages:
- You do not have to set up and run a business.
- You do not have to perform many of the tasks a publisher does.
- You can have a book published.

Disadvantages:
- Professional reviewers will not review a vanity published book.
- You pay for the book production and may pay for any marketing tasks you decide to have the publishing house perform.
- You get a payment per book somewhere between what you would get if you published via self-publishing and traditional publishing.

Chapter 1   Introduction to Publishing

Chapter 2:

Writing for Publication

Writing for Publication

We speak to aspiring writers often. Usually their dream is to write a novel or perhaps a story based on their own history. Sometimes they wish to publish their poetry. One of our first questions is "Why do you want to publish a book?". We are not being flippant. Your answer will help you decide what to write about, how to write about it, and how to produce and market it. There are three common reasons for publishing.

The first reason to write a book is for the prestige of being an author. If that is all that is important to you, then you could write about anything you want from poetry (the least commercially viable form of writing) to a cookbook (one of the most commercially viable forms of writing).

The second reason authors want to publish is to build credibility in their field of expertise. If your purpose is to establish yourself as an expert in some arena, then you will have to write a book about your topic of expertise and create some fresh insight. Often, authors who publish to build credibility are also speakers and they want to develop a book which complements their speaking topic. You can show yourself to be an expert at carpentry, business management, or any area in which you possess great skill or knowledge. This type of book will have a narrow audience, but it can be productive if tied to speaking engagements.

The third most common reason for writing books is to make money. Interestingly, the books that sell most easily are not novels or stories of any type. The most likely topics for marketable books are how-to books, cookbooks, regional travel guides, restaurant/hotel directories, and any book topic which can be serialized and published on a repeating basis with new information. Many types of books require hand selling and professional reviews, but the types of books listed earlier in this paragraph have a better chance of selling through internet marketing alone than the latest science fiction novel by I.M. Unknown. Fiction books are more difficult to market and poetry books are the most difficult books to market.

What most writers don't know about the book market

Most aspiring authors are not familiar with how the book market works. This can be a disadvantage if making money is their primary purpose in publishing. Not understanding at least some of the mechanisms which drive the book market will make it more difficult for the author to set realistic expectations and to develop a product which is marketable.

Sales to end consumers are the only sales that matter. Books sold to bookstores but not subsequently sold to consumers will be returned to the publisher. You might be excited by the number of books released to bookstores, and then six months later, find you must return your advance on royalties to your publisher because final sales figures did not meet expectations.

Book buyers, including the people who do acquisitions for libraries, are largely driven by professional reviewers and intense marketing. Celebrity status can help in the marketing and it is the reason why many publishers seem to concentrate on celebrity authors. Remember, for publishers, the goal is to make money and the chances are slim that any book will meet sales expectations.

Most book buyers walk into a store (or log onto the internet) with specific titles to purchase. These selections come from best seller lists, reviewer's columns, recommendations from friends, and school-required reading lists. Most book sales in bookstores are the result of recommendations from people the end consumer trusts.

Understanding these aspects of the book market will help you make sound decisions about how to produce and market your book.

Developing Books that Sell

If your primary purpose in creating a book is to make a return, then you will want to understand which books are most likely to turn a profit.

Non-fiction vs. Fiction: The reason we hear about best sellers is because they are so unusual. Best sellers make up less than 5% of the book market. But you do not have to have a best seller to have a profitable book. What you do need is a workable strategy. While fiction books can become bestsellers, the most likely candidate for a profitable book is a non-fiction book about a topic people want to understand better.

If you have expertise in a non-fiction area (like gardening) or are willing to find or analyze information (like a hotel directory or stock analysis), you can create a marketable book.

Think first about how you will Market your Book: To be successful with your book, before you commit a single word to paper, think about how you will market your book. For example:

- Do you intend to market on the internet? Then you will want to create a book about a topic people will be searching for using search engines.
- Do you intend to primarily market your book to libraries? You need to choose a publishing route which will get your book to professional reviewers writing for library trade journals. You will also want to have this book cataloged by the Library of Congress.
- Do you intend to attend book trade shows in order to market your books? If so, you will want to have an advertising budget to market your book. Most bookstores and distributors are not only looking at the book but also how much advertising/marketing you will be doing to promote the book.

Think about your intended audience. Include features in your book which respond to the needs of your reader and which make your book easier to market to a particular group of readers. While it may be true that many readers would benefit from your book, it is very difficult and cost-prohibitive to reach that huge population. Instead, focus your marketing effort on a definable group of readers and have word-of-mouth and later marketing campaigns reach the broader audience. Possible features you could add to enhance your book's appeal include:

- Hooks (helpful for marketing fiction works)
- Appendices
- An index
- Graphs, charts, or illustrations
- Recipes
- A glossary of topic-specific vocabulary
- Checklists
- Step-by-step instructions
- Resource Guide

Designing your book for your Primary Selling Venue: If your primary selling venue is the internet, the book cover must be easy to see in a thumbnail icon. The title should include search terms related to your book's topic so casual searching will reveal your book's title. Remember the title can include the primary title consisting of a few words and a sub-title with more clarity of the book's subject matter. To make it easy to read, the cover should have a light background color with dark printing. It is much more difficult to read white letters on a black background than the reverse.

If your primary marketing venue will be bookstores or street markets, the front cover should be intriguing and the back cover should include an interesting summary of the book, an endorsement or testimonial if you have one, an ISBN, a barcode, and the price as the minimum information. (For more complete information on developing a cover, see "Designing the Cover" in Chapter 4.) Include a brief biography on either the back cover or on the last page of the book. Place a dedication in the front matter of the book. While the dedication does not "sell" the book, many readers are curious to see to whom the book is dedicated. After years of watching how people consider a book while they are standing in a bookstore, we can tell you these are the first factors purchasers review.

Once they have reviewed the front and back cover and looked for the dedication, they may thumb through the book. Make your book easy to use. Select the correct binding. (For more information, see the section titled "Book Format and Binding Options" in Chapter 4.) The book layout needs to be clean, easy to follow, and include sufficient white space to give the reader room to breathe. Books which feel crowded or cramped, do not do well.

Useful writing tips

Hooks: Hooks are references to interests, things, and activities that readers can identify with. Hooks provide readers with a motivation for purchasing your book. They also help you market the book. Here is one example of how to use hooks. If your lead character is a golfer who works as a accountant in Seattle, then this book might be marketed through golfing pro shops, golfing magazines, accountant magazines and professional organizations, and in book and gift stores in Seattle.

Proof Again and Again: One key to producing a quality book is to have eyes other than your own read and proof your work. After a couple of readings, it is difficult to spot errors in one's own writing. Also, you may be very knowledgeable about your topic and another reviewer can point out areas in your book which might benefit from more in-depth explanations.

Consistency through Style Sheets: There are many style manuals available including Strunk and White and the Associated Press Style Manual. Each serves a different community of writers. The standard reference for book writers is the Chicago Manual of Style – all 956 pages of it! However, it is more important when writing your book, to be internally consistent on matters of punctuation and grammar usage, than to use any particular style manual.

As you develop your book, it is helpful to create a style sheet for yourself. A style sheet will help you stay consistent and lessen the number of errors in your final product. You have probably had the experience of spotting an error in a book. You will be surprised how hard you will have to work to keep errors in your own work to a minimum. Style sheets include information like:

- Number of spaces before and after ellipses
- Whether to use contractions or not
- Any point of grammar you find yourself looking up over and over again
- Correct spellings of words you commonly misspell (even with Spell Checker)
- Book formatting and typeface choices

Creating a series: If you are going to write fiction of any kind, plan to write a series. Series books perform much better than single books. This is because each new book builds readership for the previous books. Readers become familiar with your writing style and subject and are interested in following the progress of the characters they have come to know. Lots of books are very successful with a series approach. Harry Potter, of course, is a current example, but there are many others – Agatha Christie's Miss Marple and Hercule Poirot, the Nancy Drew and Hardy Boy Mystery series, Bernard Cromwell's series based on Richard Sharpe and so on.

You can also use the series idea for non-fiction topic areas. Rachel Ray's line of "30 minute meals"-based cookbooks is one example. Or think of an approach where the series is based on increasing skill level — a series of three books on beginning, intermediate, and then advanced knitting, for example. Or you can create a series by focusing on a particular part of something in each book — like the Sunset book series on landscaping for the home.

If your book will be non-fiction, think about collecting information that expires regularly. Examples of book types that meet this criteria are:

- Text books
- Directories
- Travel guides
- Non-fiction topics in rapidly changing fields.

Resources: There are many resources available to writers to help them determine their market, hone their writing skills, keep them up-to-date on the latest trends in the industry, and market their books to interested publishers. Here are a few that we have found to be particularly useful.

- **Chicago Manual of Style:** a tome which supplies the correct use of the English language
- **Writers Digest:** a magazine with tips on writing and publishing
- **Literary Market Place:** a two-volume publication listing publishers, agents, editors, addresses, and book categories
- **Publisher's Weekly:** a magazine with current information about the book market, conventions, and deals being made by the mid- and large-size publishers. Also available on-line at **www.publishersweekly.com/**.

By considering and using the aforementioned factors prior to and during the writing of your book, you will be able to create a book which is more likely to succeed no matter what your reason for publishing.

Chapter 3:

How to Work with a Subsidy Publisher

How to Work with a Subsidy Publisher

Working with a subsidy publisher makes sense for certain situations. If you are publishing for the prestige of being an author or if you wish to enhance your credibility as an expert in your field, working with a subsidy publisher could be a viable strategy. Other situations which work well with subsidy publishing are:

- Class book projects for school
- Fundraising projects
- Family history or genealogy works
- "Proof of concept" projects where you publish and sell your book with the idea of approaching a traditional publisher once you have sold over 1,000 copies.

Remember, using a subsidy publisher means you will pay the publisher to produce the book. The publisher will take the manuscript and layout the book, create a cover, have the book printed, and usually, include the book on their website. For additional fees, subsidy publishers frequently offer other services like editorial review and marketing packages.

Finding a Subsidy Publisher

Search on the internet using the keywords "self publish", "self publishing", or "publish". Subsidy publishers often emphasize "self publishing" in their advertising because many authors who want to complete their book projects do not know how to go about true self publishing or do not want to take on all the tasks that self publishing requires. The subsidy publisher provides an intermediate way to approach publishing by doing many of the functions of publishing for a fee.

Another way to find subsidy publishers is to make a trip to the local library and check their reference copy of *Literary Market Place™*. For more information on what to expect of this reference and how to use it, check out Appendix C: Book Publishing and Printing Resources.

Review the Fine Print

Once you find a couple of subsidy publishers, take the time to print off a copy of their contract and review it. Not surprisingly, there will be a lot of similarities between publishers. However, you will want to make sure you understand and have the answers to the following:

- how much you will pay for the services they will provide
- who holds the copyright of the published work
- what recurring fees there might be for keeping your book in print
- whether the book will be put into any distribution chain other than on the subsidy publisher's website (i.e. will it be listed with major online book vendors?)
- is distribution through a wholesaler like Ingram (the largest wholesaler of books in the United States) part of the package
- will libraries be able to order it through Baker &

Taylor (the primary distributor to libraries)
- the fees for additional services
- what file format the manuscript needs to be in for the publisher to process it
- will you receive a proof copy of the book as part of the fee or is it an additional fee
- how long it will take from the time you submit the file to when the book is available for printing
- how much will each copy of the book cost you, the author
- what trade discount rates will they support?

If you do not already know why these questions are important, you will find clarification in the remainder of this chapter.

Services Subsidy Publishers Provide

Subsidy publishers provide a number of services to take your manuscript to a completed book. You will want to check their contract carefully in order to make sure you know exactly what you will get for your money. Oh, did we mention this already? Yes, it **is** that important, and we **cannot stress enough** how important this is. Here are some of the functions you might see listed in a subsidy publishing contract or on their website. Some of these functions or services may be part of their basic package and others may be offered for additional fees:

- convert manuscript to book interior
- cover design
- Bookland-EAN Barcode assignment

- printing
- shipping
- delivery
- ISBN assignment
- bibliographic data submitted to ISBN agency
- wholesale distribution (usually for an additional fee)
- editorial review (usually for an additional fee)
- marketing packages (always an additional fee).

Book Layout: With some subsidy publishers you can lower the cost of your book project by doing the layout for the book interior yourself (i.e. Lulu.com). If this is appealing to you, check out the section titled "Preparing Your Manuscript for Publication as a Self Publisher" in Chapter 4 .

Cover Design: Subsidy publishers have two approaches to book covers. The first is to use a preformatted cover into which they put the critical information of your book (title, author name, and so on). The second approach is to ask the author for ideas on what the author would like to see on the cover. The first approach means the cover is easy for the publisher to generate, but it may not be reflective of the creativity you have put into your book. The second approach may be even worse for you in the end, because you may not know very much about how to create a successful cover. If you want to contribute input to the cover design check out the section titled "Designing the Cover" in Chapter 4.

Printing: All of the subsidy publishers we know of use print-on-demand technology to print their books. This means a higher unit cost than if an offset printer was used to print the book. This does not, necessarily, work against you. This, in fact, could work well for you. In order for offset printing to make sense, large numbers of books must be printed (the smallest offset print runs we have heard of are 500 books, most printers start with 1,000 books as their minimum run). These books must be inventoried, warehoused, and shipped to their final destination once ordered. If you are a new author, you will need to do an aggressive campaign to sell 1,000 books. Do not count on all of your friends and relatives who say they will buy a book once you have published it. Most likely only a small percentage of them will actually make a purchase. If you do not have a solid marketing plan, you could end up with 950 books sitting in your garage (not the best place to store books which need to be climate-controlled in order to remain in salable condition).

Access to some Distribution Channels: If you plan to sell your books to a limited number of people who you will contact directly either through a specific group you are working with (your church or a class) or through speaking engagements, you do not need to be concerned about distribution channels. If, however, you plan to market your book so customers will purchase it through internet vendors or bookstores, or so libraries will purchase it for inclusion in their collections, then you need to understand distribution channels.

The largest wholesaler of books in the United States is a company called Ingram. All roughly 25,000 bookstores purchase their books from Ingram, so it makes sense to have your book listed for distribution with Ingram. There are other wholesalers and distributors. A wholesaler usually lists available books in a database and sometimes in a printed catalog. Distributors often do some marketing for the books they carry. Wholesalers and distributors are paid a portion of the trade discount in exchange for their services. For more information on how these discounts work, see Appendix D: Trade Discounts and How They Work.

Most libraries do the bulk of their purchasing through Baker & Taylor. If your goal is to place your books in libraries, make sure your book is listed with Baker & Taylor. You will also want to consider seriously traditional publishing or self publishing as opposed to subsidy publishing. Most library buyers use library trade journals and American Library Association (ALA) conventions for sourcing their new book purchases. The library trade journals will not review books published by subsidy publishers and, often, not even self publishers. A self publisher with a large enough marketing budget may be able to attend one or more of the ALA conventions held throughout each year.

Preparing Your Manuscript for Publication with a Subsidy Publisher

We have been asked numerous times by authors to review a manuscript and, sometimes, subsidy-published books.   Our experience indicates the most obvious problem with subsidy and self published books is a lack of editing. Do yourself a favor and ask a scholarly friend to edit your work or pay a professional.   This step is often skipped. Believe me, it is hard to spot errors once you have looked at your manuscript more than twice.   Get someone else to look it over and mark down corrections, suggestions, and concerns.   Be open to the constructive criticism.   It will improve your product.

Check the publisher's criteria for submitting the manuscript.   If the publisher will be laying out the book interior, they will normally accept a text document file. Check which format the file will need to be in.   Many will accept Word documents.   PDF documents are usually only accepted if you have already done the final interior layout.

If you wish to have graphics or pictures inserted into the book interior, make sure the locations of the graphics are clear.   Also, check to see that your graphics files meet the specifications of the subsidy publisher.   The best reproductions of your graphics can only be achieved from high-quality source material.   Faded photographs look even more faded and grainy once they have been scanned, com-pressed into a .jpg file, and then, printed.   Instead, use .tif files.   Photographs of poor quality subtract value from your book.

Chapter 4:
Self Publishing

Self Publishing

This chapter will take you through everything you need to know in order to become a self publisher. You will learn each step in the publishing process and how to do most of these steps yourself so you can conserve cash flow. If you want to retain creative control over your book and see it published quickly, self publishing may be the answer. Self publishers perform all the functions of a traditional publisher from choosing what to publish through marketing the end product. Self publishing is a business. You are most likely to succeed if you approach it as you would any other business opportunity. Research your product (in this case your book) to make sure there is a market for it. Make sure you figure out a reasonable budget for producing and marketing your book and secure the funding to do so. Find out what you need to do to become a publisher and how to create a book.

Establishing Yourself as a Publisher

Amazing as it may seem, there is actually a fair amount of controversy over what can be called self publishing and what is subsidy publishing. Due to the stance of professional reviewers and others in the book trade, it is important to understand whether you fit the "true" self publishing title or if you are actually using subsidy publishing. The difference between subsidy and self publishing is often presented in a muddled manner, whether intentionally or not. Let me make things clearer.

39

If you are selling a book to bookstores or internet vendors, you need an ISBN on your book. Publishers own blocks of ISBNs. The ISBN agency defines a self publisher as "one who is undertaking the financial risk to bring a book to market and coordinating everything involved: advertising, marketing, printing, order fulfillment, etc.".

If you are only selling your books in conjunction with speaking appearances or at craft markets, then you do not need an ISBN. You may still be able to legitimately claim to be a self publisher if you do all the functions of a publisher and do not use a subsidy publisher to print your book.

If you use any of the recognized subsidy publishers, according to the book trade standards, you are not a self published author. Some of the most widely recognized subsidy publishers are listed in Appendix C: Book Publishing and Printing Resources.

Obtaining ISBNs

There are over 160 ISBN agencies worldwide. The United States Government authorizes one company, R.R. Bowker, LLC, to assign ISBNs to publishers supplying an address in the United States, U.S. Virgin Islands, Guam and Puerto Rico. The database maintained by Bowkers associates the publisher of record with a specified prefix. After the ISBN agency assigns ISBNs to a publisher, that publisher cannot resell, re-assign, transfer, or split its list of ISBNs among other publishers. The ISBN identifies not only the specific product to which it is assigned, but also the publisher to be contacted for ordering purposes. R.R. Bowker, in addition to running the distribution of ISBNs, also produces *Books in Print*™and *Book Wire*™. The company is often referred to simply as Bowkers.

Bowkers recommends you estimate the number of your publishing projects for the next 5 years and select the block which suits your needs. To apply for a block of ISBNs, go to: **http://www.isbn.org/standards/home/index.asp**

ISBNs are priced according to the number of ISBNs purchased and the required turn-around time to the publisher. You will save money if you can wait for 15 days to receive your ISBNs. The fees include both the combined processing fees and registration fees. The fee structure as of our publication date is:

REGULAR PROCESSING
(15 business day turnaround)
10 ISBNs: $275.00
100 ISBNs: $995.00
1000 ISBNs: $1,750.00

PRIORITY PROCESSING
(48 business hours turnaround)
10 ISBNs: $375.00
100 ISBNs: $1,095.00
1000 ISBNs: $1,850.00

EXPRESS PROCESSING
(24 business hours turnaround)
10 ISBNs: $400.00
100 ISBNs: $1,120.00
1000 ISBNs: $1,875.00

It is now possible to purchase single ISBNs. There are two possible ways to do so. The first way is purchase the ISBN directly from Bowkers through a new service called MyIdentifiers.com which sells single ISBNs for $125.

An alternative is to work with one of the handful of companies with which R.R. Bowker has entered into agreements allowing the company to submit official applications for single ISBNs on behalf of the self publishers and authors with whom they work. These companies have agreed to provide special programs under which an ISBN can be assigned by the US ISBN Agency.

If an ISBN is purchased from a company other than R.R. Bowker or through the special programs of the companies listed here, that ISBN will not identify you as the publisher of your title. You will have published through a subsidy publisher. The twelve companies authorized to complete the single ISBN application are:

Aardvark Global Publishing Company	Lulu.com
	PPC Books
Bethany Press	Publisher Services
Espressio	RJ Communications
FilmMasters	RKD Press
Instantpublisher.com	Signature Books
	WordClay

The Book Development Process

It is wise for a publisher to use a checklist containing the steps to work through when taking a book from concept to completed project. This process can take anywhere from 6 months to 2 years. This is our list of steps. Feel free to modify the process to suit your needs. If you find unfamiliar publishing terms in this list, please check the glossary. This list is numbered to indicate sequence.

1. Identify book concept.
2. Contract author and set deadlines and publication date.
3. Initial editing.
4. Determine binding and trim size and get templates from printer.
5. Assign ISBN to project.
6. Contract for illustrations if necessary.
7. Initial book layout.
8. Second round of editing.
9. Develop front and back matter.
10. Insert front and back matter into book.
11. Insert artwork into book layout.
12. Submit application for Library of Congress Control Number.
13. Final editing.
14. Develop cover.
15. Edit cover.
16. Prepare text block (book interior) and cover files for printer.
17. Submit to printer. Order initial print run.
18. Send out press releases and initial marketing

announcing upcoming book release.

19. Load book information onto our website.

20. Schedule book signings.

21. Review proof. If acceptable, release book to distribution.

22. Register book with *Books in Print*™ and other databases.

23. Once initial print run is received, submit copyright application and fulfill Library of Congress Preassigned Control Number requirements.

24. Continue marketing book.

Finding an Illustrator

Many artists are interested in illustrating books, but have never done so. Book illustration has particular requirements and you may need to work closely with the illustrator to make sure these requirements are met. We suggest reviewing samples of their work or asking several artists to submit character concepts for your story. Choose an artist who can produce a style of drawing which complements your story. There are three ways to find an illustrator for your book.

- Let friends and acquaintances know you are looking for an illustrator. When using this approach, you will probably find many interested artists most of whom have never illustrated a book before. Be ready to spend extra time working with an artist who is illustrating a book for the first time.

- Use the search terms "book illustrator", "children's illustrator", and "picture book artists" to find resources on the internet.

– There are also two associations for book illustrators which may be able to help you find an artist: The Picture Book Artists Association and The Society of Children's Book Writers and Illustrators. Check their respective websites for the most current contact information.

Be prepared to work with your selected artist. In order for the pictures to be correctly placed, the artist will need to know what size the pages will be and what the bleed area will be. The easiest way to supply the necessary information is to give your illustrator the template of the book interior from the printer. You will need to have selected your trim size and binding in order to get the correct template from the printer.

We also strongly recommend a written contract which includes the number of illustrations, specifications for the form of submitted artwork (either original art or computer graphics file), a detailed timeline for the project including a deliverables schedule, payment specification, transfer of copyright, how the artist will be credited in the book, and an artist warranty that the artwork does not infringe on any intellectual property rights or violate any laws. Provide the illustrator with the printer templates and a marked copy of the manuscript showing where the illustrations will appear. If you have an idea of what you would like to have illustrated on each page, write a short description of the picture so the illustrator knows what you have in mind.

The contract helps you and the illustrator understand the requirements of the job and keeps your book on its production schedule. Having illustrations delivered in small groups supplies you an early opportunity to make sure the artwork fits the page layout and your book concept. Any changes can be worked out immediately and the artist will be able to apply the new information to the rest of the project.

Finding a Printer

There are three basic options for printing books. The first option is to hand-make the book. You can do this yourself as a craft project. Search the internet on "making a book" or "make a book by hand". You would only want to do this for a small number of books. If your strategy is to sell at high-end craft fairs or fine art fairs (if you do a beautiful leather-bound edition, for instance), producing quality hand-made books may work.

The second option is to use an offset printer. An offset printer is a good choice if you know you can sell over 1,000 books, are willing to deal with inventory, and have the money to invest in the print run. Find an offset printer by using the Print Industry Exchange at **http://www.printindustry.com/** which posts your job to printers around the world who will submit quotes to you. Read more about offset printers in Appendix C: Book Publishing and Printing Resources. Four to eight weeks is the normal turn-around time for an offset-print project. There are a few offset printers who may offer a two-week turn-around depending on the timing of your job.

The third option is a print-on-demand printer. Choose this option if you have a restricted printing budget, desire a small or no inventory to manage, or are not sure how many books will sell within a year. This option also works well for backlist books. You can always do an offset print run if you have a large order. Appendix C: Book Publishing and Printing Resources provides search terms and example print-on-demand printers.

Setting the Book's Retail Price

Determining what the retail price should be for your book involves a little bit of accounting and a little bit of art. To be profitable, the book price must exceed the cost of producing the book. Add up the cost of any rights payments you have made, the book set-up fees, the print cost for the initial print run, catalogue fees, proof fees, any professional services provided for the book (illustrator, editor, copyeditor, book designer, cover designer, etc), etc. Divide this number by the number of books in the initial print run to get an estimated cost of production per book.

In theory, you should also add a percentage of the overhead costs for your business to the cost of production. Determining the overhead costs and deciding on the percentage of the overhead costs which should be allocated to your book can be difficult for the first-time publisher. One approach is to include all your known costs in the aforementioned calculation. This approach will most probably make your production costs look quite high. The resulting price tag for each book would be correspondingly high, making it difficult to sell the book. An alternative approach is to leave out the overhead costs while calculating production costs for pricing purposes. After you have calculated your anticipated income per book, divide the overhead costs by the anticipated income to find out how many books you would have to sell to cover your overhead costs.

Before you set your retail price, research the price of other books similar to your own. Find out what the retail prices are for these books. Make sure you are comparing appropriate books. If your book will be a perfect bound, all-black-ink-interior novel, find books printed the same way and about the same general topic.

Compare the price range of these books to your estimated cost of production. You do not want to overprice your book. You will sell very few books if your book is seriously out of line with books of similar quality . Hopefully, you will find the prices of these comparable books larger than your estimated production costs. The cost of production should be no more than about 30% of the anticipated retail price. This is because you will also have to pay the wholesaler, distributor, bookstore, and royalties with this money. What's left after that is your profit.

If you find your anticipated profit unsatisfactory, analyze your production costs. Carefully examine all costs and the possible changes you can make in order to minimize the production cost. Can you do any additional work yourself to lower costs? Can you find a better deal on the printing cost by using a different printer? Can you lower the cost by removing color from the interior of the book, reducing the page count, changing the binding, and so on?

Another strategy is to eliminate the wholesaler, distributor, and bookstore from your distribution network. In this scenario, you handle all the distribution. You can do this by ordering short runs from your printer. Advertise the book on your website and process all orders directly. Set up speaking engagements or other book signing events and bring your own inventory to sell. Offer your book through barbershops, clubs, hair salons, or any other sales venue that fits your marketing strategy.

The accounting part of setting a retail price can be challenging because you are new to publishing and you are not familiar with all the costs involved. However, the art part of pricing is even more ambiguous and difficult to grasp. This is when you try to divine what a customer is willing to pay for the type of book you are creating. The best approach is researching the pricing of similar books as mentioned earlier. If you do not price your book in that range, you will have difficulty competing with the other books in your category.

Obtaining a Library of Congress Preassigned Control Number (PCN)

The Library of Congress assigns control numbers in advance of publication to those titles that may be added to the Library's collections. Librarians can use the number to search the national databases and order catalog cards from the Library of Congress or commercial suppliers. The PCN program is available to United States publishers only. Publishers must list a U.S. place of publication on the title or copyright page. Books can still be printed overseas, but the publisher has to be located in the U.S.

This program was primarily designed for small publishers. Larger publishers use the Cataloging in Publication program. There are a number of circumstances under which you do not need a PCN assigned. The most common exceptions are:

– eBooks
– Books not intended for wide library distribution
– Mass market paperbacks
– Serials (periodicals, journals, annuals, and other publications issued regularly; contact the National Serials Data Program for assignment of an International Standard Serial Number (ISSN))
– Textbooks below the college level
– Expendable educational materials
– Items under 50 pages except genealogies and children's literature.

To sign up for the program and register your book, go to the Library of Congress Preassigned Control Number Program home page on the internet. Searching on the terms "library of congress pcn" or "pcn loc" will return the home page address.

You will need to submit your application for a PCN before you complete your book since the number must be printed on the copyright page. It normally takes about a week to receive the number. To complete your registration, you must mail a copy of the finished book to the Library of Congress. This program is separate from the copyright program. You will end up sending two copies of your book to complete the copyright process for a total of three books to the Library of Congress. However, each program has a unique address and different paperwork trails. The copyright process is described in a later section of this chapter.

Preparing Your Manuscript for Publication as a Self Publisher

The next nine sections of this chapter take you through the physical process and decisions of preparing your manuscript for publication. Use this information in conjunction with your checklist for publication. Do not forget the steps addressing the editing of your manuscript. Editing is very important. If you need a professional editor, you can find one by searching the internet on "editor for hire" or "editor services". At the very least, remember to run spell-check and grammar check. These programs do not find everything and cannot provide fact checking, logical analysis, style tips, or content analysis, but at least they can help you eliminate some of the most obvious errors which seem to creep into every manuscript. A review by a good editor is invaluable.

Determining Book Trim Size: Trim size is the size of the book once the excess paper has been cut away by the printer. There are some common trim sizes that most printers offer and then there are sizes which are so infrequently used that only a few printers offer them. When you are thinking about your book in its concept phase, think about the category of the book and what distribution channels you will use. The category of the book will often help you decide what trim size and binding type is suitable. For example, if you are writing a book for children between the ages of 4 to 6 years old, the trim size is often large (7 X 10 inches or 8.5 X 11 inches). As another example, if you are writing a novel for the paperback trade, the usual trim size is 6 X 9 inches.

One way to get more information about the trim sizes and binding types most frequently used for the category of book you wish to publish is to go to a library or bookstore and measure the books in the category. The reasons you will want to consider the trim sizes currently in use for your category of book are the expectation of the consumer, the ease of use by the consumer, and the expectations and ease of handling by the distribution chain. If you are producing a novelty book for sale in a gift shop, then you may wish to consider odd trim sizes.

Book Format and Binding Options: Books can be printed in hardcover, softcover, or distributed as e-books. Each book format release requires a separate ISBN.

Each printer will have equipment that produces several different formats, sizes, and binding types of books. If you are self publishing, you select these features for your book and obtain the printer's templates for the book interior and cover design.

One consideration for selecting a book format is your intended audience and their anticipated use of the book. If you are producing books for the purpose of making money, another consideration has to be whether or not the books will show a profit.

Hardcover books are more durable than any other book format and are useful for reference books which do not change frequently, books for young children, and books for hard use situations (i.e. in the workshop or kitchen).

Hardcover books can be leather-bound, boxed (in slipcases), cloth-bound, case laminate, dust jacketed, or plastic. The most common types are case laminate and cloth-bound with a dust jacket. Case laminate refers to a cover made of cardboard covered with heavy, slick paper printed with a 4- or 5-color process. The binding can be mechanical (spiral bound or comb), glue, or glue and stitching.

Not surprisingly, hardcover books are more expensive to produce than softcover books. Most traditional publishers produce the initial release of a book in hardcover then later release a paperback version. Since they use offset printers and print large runs, they have the advantage of economy of scale. Small publishers often do not have the budget for a large print run nor the ability to store or move the amount of product necessary to make a profit on a hardcover book printed through an off-set print run.

Softcover or paperback books work well in most situations and are the standard for "trade" books. (Trade books are books intended to market through bookstores.) The covers of most paperback books are glued to the text block of the book. The glue binding is called "Perfect Bound". They can also be stitched or saddle-stitched. They are less expensive to produce than hardcover books. For small publishers, paperback books are more likely to turn a profit since retail prices can be set at levels the consumer will pay.

eBooks are a particularly suitable selection for reaching high-tech users with informational books because of the search features included in an eBook. Publishing eBooks is still in its infancy and, as a result, information on how to do it changes rapidly. To release an eBook, you will need either the software necessary to create the correctly formatted eBook or an eBook publisher or printer. Find an eBook publisher by searching the internet with the term "eBook publisher". Some of the listings will be publishers (they own the ISBN) and others will actually be printers (you supply the ISBN).

Currently, each eBook reader operates uniquely, accepting a defined set of formats. Unfortunately, the industry does not have a single format for eBooks. The three biggest format contenders are Amazon.com's Kindle reader, Adobe's PDF-based Electronic Book Exchange (EBX), and EPUB which is an open source solution set by the International Digital Publishing Forum. There are also a number of lesser known solutions. The publishing industry is more or less moving in the direction of the EPUB standard which allows lines of text to flow differently to fit the varying sizes of smaller screens. But, we are not there yet.   Many eBook reading devices currently support HTML with the prominent exception of the Sony reader.   Another widely accepted format by reading devices is PDF with the notable exception of Amazon's Kindle reader.

For the customer this means there is no guarantee that a particular title will be available in a particular format. For you, the publisher, this means making a decision about which format you will use to have your book published. The particular format you select will determine which distribution channels are open to you. For instance, if you choose to publish your book so it can be read on a Kindle reader, only people who have a Kindle reader will be able to read your book and probably the only places which will offer it for download are Amazon.com and your own web-site. You could, of course, always choose to produce the book in two eBook formats so it could be read through more reading devices.

Using the Printer's Templates: Printers provide templates in different ways. Some will provide PDF files with an annotated drawing depicting the margins, bleed area, gutter, and any other guidance on layout they wish to note. The drawings can be imported into your book layout software allowing you to lay the book elements (text and graphics, if any) over the drawing or use the measurements from the diagram directly in your book layout software.

Other printers provide a set of measurements which you then enter into your computer software.

In order to obtain the correct template, you will need to specify the trim size of your book, the binding, and the paper for the book interior, if the printer offers options for that. You will need to determine the number of pages in your book before you can download the cover template because the cover template normally includes the spine. The width of the spine will vary based on the number of interior pages. Download both the book interior and the cover template.

If your book is text only in the interior, then the simplest and least expensive way to lay out your book is with Microsoft Word. Once you have created the Word document, you will need to convert it to a PDF file. Most printers will accept such, but you will want to check with your selected printer on any specifics for the PDF file. Many printers can only work with PDF files which have been converted using Adobe Acrobat Distiller in the PDFX-1a:2001 format option. Check before you create your file.

The two premier book design software packages are Quark XPress and Adobe's InDesign CS4. Both are accepted by book printers in their native file formats so once you have created the book, there is no need to do a conversion to another file format. These programs permit much more sophisticated book layout options. If you are working with many illustrations or other graphics in your book, you may want to seriously consider these software packages. MS Word has limitations on how many graphics it can handle and what can be done with them. At the time of the production of this book, these software packages cost $800 and $700 respectively.

Another option for laying out the book is to use MS Publisher. While designed primarily for commercial printing of brochures and other business literature, it can stretch to do book layout. If you have the MS Office Professional package, you have both Word and Publisher, so this may be an option. Since Publisher files are not accepted in their native file format by book printers, these files must also be converted to the PDF format as mentioned with relation to MS Word.

Be sure to follow the printer's template precisely. Printers will not process files which do not meet their criteria. Avoid the time-wasting activity of re-doing your work. Gutter spaces must be left blank. If you want to have color to the edge of a page, you must run the color all the way through the bleed area. The bleed area allows for the slight variance that occurs during the trimming process. This is true for both the interior and the cover. Even if you choose a black and white interior, where the bleed area is not a concern, you will most likely have a cover in color. Do not forget to carry your color through the bleed area on the cover.

Developing Front Matter: The pages before the start of the text of your book make up what is called, "front matter". Front matter creates a transition from the cover to the heart of your book. Between front and back matter, you also have an opportunity to meet the signature requirement of the printer. If needed, you can insert blank pages to meet the signature requirement.

If you decide to print a hardcover book, the inside of the hardcover and the first piece of paper are called, "end paper". End paper is usually made of thicker paper than the paper used for the actual text block. Although most frequently plain white, end papers can also be printed with fancy designs. Paperback books do not have end paper.

Here is a list of several types of pages which you may wish to include in the front matter. The order listed indicates the normal order in which these pages occur. You do not need to include all of these pages in every book. Choose the ones that apply and help you meet the printer's signature requirement.

- *"Praises for"*. Although not often seen in hardcover books, many paperbacks include a page or two of favorable quotes from reviewers before any other information. If you have gathered such quotes you can use them here or on the back cover. Place the quote in quotation marks and list the source.
- *Half-Title*. The half-title page is usually the first printed page and lists only the title. It will be a right hand page.
- *Frontispiece*. A left hand page opposite from the Title Page with an illustration only.
- *Title Page*. The title page lists the title, author(s) (or editor, translator, re-teller), illustrator, and publisher. Normally a right hand page.

- *Copyright Page.* This page is required. It is normally a left hand page immediately following the Title Page. More specific information on the copyright page follows this listing.
- *Dedication.* If there is a dedication, it should be alone on the page facing the copyright page.
- *Acknowledgements.* Acknowledgements might be included on either the copyright page or the dedication page if you are pressed for space. Ideally, acknowledgements will be made on a separate right hand page.
- *Table of Contents.* A Table of Contents is a useful addition to educational or informational books. You may also wish to include one if you wrote a book of fiction with chapter titles. Start the Table of Contents on a right hand page. Continue for as many pages as needed.
- *Listing of Illustrations.* A listing of all illustrations and the pages on which they appear.
- *Listing of previous titles by the author.* A partial or full listing of previously published titles by the author. Arrangement of the titles can be alphabetical, by date of publication (either most recent to first title or the reverse), by topic matter, or by lead character if you have written more than one series. This page can occur prior to the Half-title or in the back matter.

You must include a copyright page in the front matter. Take a look at the copyright page at the front of this book for an example of how one should look. The copyright page must include:

- a copyright notice,
- the title,
- the author name,
- the ISBN,
- the publishing company name,
- an "All rights reserved." statement,
- the Library of Congress Pre-assigned Control Number if you have one (note: large publishers will insert Cataloging in Publication Data here),
- if you have a Pre-assigned Control Number, you must include a statement "Printed in" and the town and state of the publisher.

The copyright notice should be in the following format: Copyright (year or publication), (Name of copyright holder). A completed notice would look like this:

Copyright 2009, I.M. Author

Other information you might include on the copyright page includes:
- any credits for the book designer, cover designer, and photographer
- the contact information for the publishing company,
- the website address for the publishing company or author,
- a permission statement which tells readers what, if anything, you allow them to do with your copyrighted material or if they need to contact you to seek permission.

Examples of permission statements include:

- "No part of this book may be reproduced in any way."
- "No part of this book may be used or reproduced in any manner without written permission except in the case of brief quotations embodied in critical articles and reviews. For permission contact..."
- "For information about permission to reproduce selections from this book, write to..."
- "Educators may reproduce the worksheets in this book for use in their classrooms."
- "Readers may reproduce the pattern worksheets for their own use only."

Laying out the Text Block: Start the text block of your book on a right hand page and number that page "one." If you decide to use numbering in the front matter use roman numerals and start the numbering on the page immediately following the copyright page. Use the template you obtain from the printer to set the page margins.

Choose a typeface which is easy to read. Typefaces with serifs are more easily read for longer periods of time than typefaces without serifs (sans serif). Examples of good typefaces for the text block are:

Century   Century Schoolbook   Garamond

Palatino Linotype   Times New Roman

All the samples here are sized at 12 points. You can see there are differences in the resulting appearance of these letters even though the font size is the same. When you are selecting the font, consider the reader. Most adults are comfortable reading 10, 11, or 12 point fonts. The 12 point size being more comfortable for readers over 40. Books using typefaces larger than a 12 point size qualify as "Large Print" texts. We have used Palatino Linotype in 12 point font for the regular text this book.

Children's books are most often in a large print size. Try font sizes of 20 to 26 for the interior text of a children's book.

Another important factor to consider when selecting the typeface is how many pages the text block will be. This is important because more pages means a higher printing charge per book. Compare the typeface Garamond to Palatino Linotype on the previous page and you can easily see a text block done in Garamond will be shorter than one done in Palatino Linotype.

Chapter headings, section headings, and other short pieces of text designed to capture attention or provide a natural break in rhythm to the text can be in a sans serif text. The eye naturally spends longer on sans serif text because the serif which provides the connection from one letter to another letter is not present. Examples of sans serif typefaces which work well as breaks for the text include:

Arial Black   **Franklin Gothic Heavy**
Tahoma   **Tahoma Small Cap**   Verdana

Another technique you can use with your text block is to create atmosphere for the book by your choice in typeface. A book instantly feels Oriental when you use Papyrus, or humorous with **Comic Sans MS**, girlie with Curlz MT, or elegant with French Script MT. Use unusual typefaces sparingly since they tend to be hard to read for extended periods.   Consider these typefaces for drop capitals, chapter headings, the title on the cover, and in the front matter.

Be consistent in your paragraph spacing and the way you treat any special text.   The idea is to create a harmonious feel to the book. Your attention to these details increase the reader's ability to move happily through the text. And, while the layout and typeface choices will not make up for a boring plot line and insipid writing, these choices can make the difference between a book which readers find innately satisfying and one they feel uncomfortable reading.

Finally, include white space on each page. Dense coverage of a page makes the book seem cramped and hard to read and digest. You might be thinking "I'll lower my printing charges by cramming everything into the page." Meanwhile the reader is thinking "I can't read this. It is too difficult." Give the reader's eyes room to travel. Make it easy to find important material by providing space between paragraphs, chapter and section headings, and around illustrations, charts, and graphs.

Including Illustrations: If charts and graphs will make the presentation of your text material easier to understand, you should include them. Make sure you allow sufficient space around each one so they are easy to read. Label the parts clearly. Also include a title for each one for clarity when you refer to it in the text. Include a short caption summarizing its information.

Photographs must be very high quality to print well. Therefore, obtain the best original photograph available, and then scan it at a resolution of a least 300dpi (dots per inch). When you insert the photograph into your book layout, it should be in TIF format rather than a JPEG or GIF format. This is because the JPEG and GIF file formats use compression techniques to make the file sizes smaller. The compression causes the resulting image to have less resolution than an image that has not been compressed. The resulting printed image looks grainy and less clear than the original. TIF files retain all data related to the photograph and will result in a better printed image. Most photographs will benefit from a caption describing the subject in the photograph and a comment about the event or setting.

Using black and white for both the photographs and the interior book layout will be less expensive than using color therefore allowing you to price your book reasonably. Currently print-on-demand books must be either all black and white or all color in the interior. Color printing is significantly more expensive and can price you right out of your intended market. You could do a color offset print run for less cost per book than print-on-demand, but then you have more upfront costs and a storage issue.

If you are including original artwork in your book, the easiest way to incorporate it is to scan it and then insert it into your interior text block. When you commission the artwork, be sure to provide your selected artist with the printer's template for the interior of the book. I know I've talked of this before but some points are so important, they deserve several mentions.

If the illustration is intended to cover the page all the way to the cut edges, the artwork must be inserted so it covers the bleed area noted on the printer's template. Since the bleed area is basically a built-in tolerance for the trimming machine, illustration material in the bleed area may or may not show up in every copy of the book. Therefore, any material in the bleed area should not be critical to the support the artwork provides to the text.

Take the time to discuss your project with the artist. Be clear about where you would like to add illustrations and what those illustrations should include. You also want to find an artist whose style of art complements the text. Read the section in this chapter on **Finding an Illustrator** ideas on finding a suitable match.

One thing we have had to double check and correct on artwork has been the quality of the scan. Often scanners will gray the background or put a line down one side of the illustration. Cleanup the background with photo processing software like Adobe's PhotoShop.

Developing Back Matter: At the conclusion of your text block, you have the option to include more pages. These pages and the material they contain are called, "back matter". Back matter should be carefully considered by the author. You can add value to your creation with the right back matter. You do not have to include all the possible types of back matter. Pick those which add to the usefulness of your book. You may also need to add a few pages to fill out the book's signature requirement. Here are possible types of back matter.

- *Appendices.* Appendices are particularly useful if your main text is informational in nature. Scholarly works, teaching texts, reference texts, and historical novels all have the possibility of benefiting from appendices which expand on the material in the main text.
- *Notes.* If you have researched your main text material or are quoting others, a notes section which provides brief expansions of the material in the text can be helpful to the reader.
- *Bibliography.* Providing additional reading on the subjects covered in your book is often a very useful feature particularly for scholarly or reference works.
- *Index.* Being able to find information in a book quickly and easily is a feature much sought after in any type of reference book including cookbooks.
- *Glossary.* Glossaries can be very useful in books on topics that have distinct vocabularies which may be unfamiliar to the average reader. For example, books on gardening, finance, computer use, carpentry, and knitting all have unique words which are not often used in ordinary conversation. Explaining these words clearly is an excellent addition to the book.

- *Resource listing.* Readers may wish to find equipment, services, or products mentioned in your book. Make that easy by providing a resource list.
- *Credits.* If you have included photographs, graphs, charts, or illustrations created by others and have not given credit elsewhere in your book, you may include a credits page in the back matter.
- *Offers from the publisher.* If the publisher has any special deals to offer readers, those deals can be offered in the back matter. Examples of the type of deal you might offer are coupons toward the purchase of the next book, a chapter from the next book, fundraising program details, and publisher or author website features.
- *Author and illustrator biographies.* If biographical information about the author and the illustrator has not been included on the back cover or jacket, include them on the last available page prior to the end paper. Most book buyers look for these biographies at the end of a book. They do not need to be long, a short paragraph is sufficient. They can include training or college degrees, awards, a mention of where they currently live, hobbies, or any other information which allows the reader to connect with the author and illustrator.
- *Blank pages.* As in front matter, blank pages can be inserted to meet signature requirements or to provide "breathing space" before the reader must put the book down and re-enter the real world.

Designing the Cover: The cover of a book is of utmost importance. Book buyers decide whether or not to read a book based on the cover and they decide quickly. In fact, research shows the average reader spends at most 8 seconds on the front cover and 15 seconds on the back. Covers must be compelling, concise, and informative.

The front cover must have the title and the name of the author. Most covers also include some sort of artwork to indicate the book type and to grab the reader's attention. If you plan to sell the book primarily through the Internet, make the cover as simple as possible so when it is displayed as a small icon on the computer screen, it is still identifiable. Pay particular attention to the title. You should be able to discern easily the letters from the background.

The back cover has more information than the front cover. Readers almost always check the price before reading anything else and they look for it here. A short blurb summarizing the book helps readers decide if they are interested. If the book is non-fiction, consider including a list of the major points covered. State the book category. This makes it easier for librarians and book sellers to shelve the book correctly.

Include the ISBN and barcode on a white background so it can be read correctly by cash register scanners. Barcodes are often supplied by printers, sometimes for free. You can also buy barcodes from Bowkers—the same company which sells ISBNs.

Consider including the publisher's name and website or contact information. You may also wish to include an illustration on the back cover which continues the theme of the front cover.

Finally, as an alternative to including the author's biography in the book's back matter, you may wish to place it and a photograph on the back cover.

Finalizing the Book for Submission to the Printer: Once you have your book interior laid out and the cover completed, you need to do final preparations for submitting your work to the chosen printer. If you have used Quark or InDesign software to complete the layout, you will only need to upload your files to the printer. Check to see what naming convention your printer requires and change the names of your files accordingly. Most printers will accept files through FTP (File Transfer Protocol) or from a storage device like a CD. There will also be a form to fill out with your contact information, method of sending the files, file names, and payment as required by the printer.

If the printer accepts PDF file formats and that is the file type you plan to submit, you need to ascertain which PDF format is required. Although some printers may accept a "Standard" format file, most require files to be in PDF/X-1a:2001 because it contains all the information commercial printers need in order to correctly print the files. Many free versions of software for creating PDF files do not have the capability to produce this type of file. The only program I know of which can create this particular file format is the definitely not free — Adobe Acrobat Distiller.

Set the dots per inch (dpi) for 300. Lower dpi settings result in poor quality reproductions and most commercial printers of books will not accept files created with lower settings. It is not worth setting the dots per inch higher, however, because the resulting file sizes are huge and there is no noticeable increase in the quality of the finished product.

Most books which contain only text and perhaps a few small graphics files can be handled easily by both a word processing program and a PDF-making program. However, if you have a file with a number of graphics files, particularly if the graphics are in color, you may run into problems with either the word processing program or the PDF-making software due to the relative file size of the book. This has happened to us with the full-color-illustration children's books we produce. Most printers will accept multiple files for the book's interior, but will appreciate having as few files as possible. To create a single file, first divide the book into sections so the word processing software can process the files. Next, using Adobe Acrobat Professional, form the PDF files for each section. Finally, combine the sections by using the option under "Create PDF" to create from multiple files.

Copyrighting Your Book

Intellectual works are covered by copyright law as soon as you create them. In theory, all you have to do is keep a record of your work, preferably with dates noted on the work, to help you prove you are the original creator. In practice, if your copyright is questioned, it is easier to support your legal case if you have registered the copyright with the Library of Congress. Registration requires a fee ($45 as we are writing this), a completed form and two copies of the "best" edition of the work within three months of publication. The "best" edition refers to the type of book produced, for instance, a hardback book is better than a paperback.

Information on filing for copyright, including the forms, is available at **http://www.copyright.gov/**. Or search the internet for "copyright" or "copyright office" to find a link to the U.S. Copyright Office which governs the program.

Please note that the Library of Congress Pre-assigned Control Number (PCN) also requires a book deposit. In the case of the PCN program, one book must be submitted to complete the program obligation. This program is separate from the copyright program.

Registering Your Book with *Books in Print*™ and other databases

Once your book is ready for booksellers and customers to order it, you will want to have it listed in *Books in Print*™. As an accredited publisher, you have an account with Bowkers. You bought your ISBNs there and are listed in their database as a publisher. You can now visit their *Books in Print*™ page, click on *Publisher*, and sign in. You will then be able to enter information about your new book. You can even upload a picture of the cover.

Another place you may wish to register your book is with the *Small Press Record of Books in Print* by Dustbooks.   Dustbooks is the leading supplier of information about small presses. Search on the term "dustbooks" to find the homepage and register as a small press publisher.

The internet offers a variety of websites where authors can connect with readers. A current example is "filedby.com". Search the internet on the term "author directory" to find other websites.

Chapter 4   Self Publishing

Chapter 5:
Selling Your Book

Selling your Book

If you thought writing your book was hard and laying it out for the printer was challenging, just wait. The hardest part of the book process is selling it. If you are working with a publisher, you will get some help in the marketing of your book. Perhaps they will set up interviews or book signings. The publisher will definitely list it in their catalog and on their website. But to really make a book fly off the shelf, the author will need to be personally involved in the marketing. This is especially true if you are self publishing because you now have to do the work of the publisher as well as the writer.

Selling your book starts when you write it

If your goal in writing a book is to make money, you need to have this goal foremost in your mind from the very beginning of the writing process. Even before you choose what to write about, you should be researching what buyers are interested in buying. This applies to all categories of books. Let us say your research shows that cookbooks sell best. If further research shows cookbooks with quick, easy meals sell best of all, then you should be heating up your skillet and testing recipes for inclusion in your planned release of "Quick and Simple Cooking that Tastes Great!".

If you want to write fiction, you should pay attention to what types of fiction books are selling and fine-tune your book concept based on the results of your research. Think about hooks for your book and how you might reach the market where those hooks apply.

Developing a marketing plan before you finish the book and why that is important

Most writers approach book writing from the perspective of their own creativity — I have this story in me and I want to share it with the world. It is a totally different perspective to come at the idea of writing a book from the sales and marketing angle.

You want to have thought about and decided on the steps you need to take to market your book. You will want to have a clear idea of what you will do to bring the book to the attention of the media, bookstores, libraries, and buyers. It will help to lay out on paper the things you will do and the timing of the steps you plan to enact.

The first six months of your book's release is critical to the marketing. Most buyers want something new. For books "New Release" may mean published within the last year, but generally it means published within the last six months. In order for you to bring your book to the attention of buyers in that short period, you need to have the plan ready to go the moment your book comes off the presses, if not before.

Here are some ideas you may wish to include in your marketing plan. You do not need to include all of them. Think about what fits you as a person and your schedule.

- Speaking engagements
- Book signings
- Website

- Blog
- Interviews on radio and TV
- Press release(s)
- School visits
- Advertising
- Article Marketing
- Submission to reviewers
- Submission to award programs
- Car trunk sales
- Charitable gifting (with press coverage)
- Review copy distribution

Once you have decided on your plan, get your marketing activities moving. Start contacting bookstores to schedule book signings, send press releases to local media, get your website built, start blogging.

What to include on the Book Cover to help sell the book

Your book itself is a marketing tool. Think about that as you develop the cover and the front and back matter. The cover and the information on it is critical to the buyer's decision to purchase your book.

Naturally the book cover should have the title and the name of the author, but there are other things you can include on the cover which help a buyer decide whether or not to buy the book. An interesting graphic which attracts the buyer's attention is useful on the front cover. When choosing graphics for the cover think of the type of book you have written . Is the book a romantic novel? Is it a business manual? Is it a cookbook? Look at the covers of other books in the genre you have written. While you will want a picture or artwork which reflects your unique work, you also want readers to recognize immediately what type of book it is. Choose artwork which is similar in approach or subject matter to other books in your genre, but unique enough to be clearly new material.

The spine should have the title, author name, and publishing company. Some cover designers have artwork continued on the spine. This is helpful in creating a mood, but should not interfere with a reader's ability to read the book title and author name easily. If the artwork on the spine is too distracting, try using a color instead of a picture.

The back cover is very important. Here you can give the reader helpful information on why choosing your book is in their best interest. Include a concise book summary. If your book is "how to" or informational in nature, make sure you list the most important information people will learn by reading your book. Make sure you list the price, the ISBN, and the barcode. Buyers check the price in the first few seconds of their review of the back cover. If they cannot find it easily, they will often put that book down and move on to another book.

Writing a Book Summary

A good book summary gives the reader an accurate idea of what to expect in the book. Misleading hype just creates disappointed readers, not devoted fans. Keep the book summary brisk. For works of fiction a paragraph or two is sufficient. For non-fiction works, write a brief summary paragraph and then a "bullet-ized" list of the features or material covered in the book.

If your book is intended for children, you may wish to include a suggested age range of readers. There are two schools of thought on listing an age range. One school of thought is that listing a suggested age range limits the reader pool when there are children who might very well enjoy the book but do not fit the age range printed on the book. On the other hand, parents almost always ask the age range for which the book is written. They are interested in making sure the content is suitable to their child's age range. Some are interested in the reading level. They want to choose either material which will challenge their young reader or reading material they know their child will be able to handle.

The book summary can be placed on the back cover of your book and also in the various directory listings in which your book will appear.

Listing the Book with Internet Vendors

You will, of course, want to list your book with Internet vendors and on your own website. Vendors use the data from the wholesaler's database. This data originates from you. You will enter it when you set up your book for printing. Make sure you have your category selected and book summary written before you submit your book for printing since this data will be requested during the set-up process for the print order.

Some printers include listings with Internet vendors as part of their printing package; others charge an additional fee for the service. Make sure you understand your printing contract.

While the listing write-up is important, listing a book with an Internet vendor does not sell your book. It provides a way for buyers to obtain your book easily once they know they need it. Your marketing efforts must include ways to reach readers directly and persuade them of the value of your book.

Developing a Book Promotion Website

Many authors and publishing companies have websites to help readers learn about the books they offer. Websites are just one way to reach readers and provide them with more information about the book and about you, the author. People like to feel connected to authors. They want to know how you conceived of writing the book, what your motivation was, where did your ideas came from, was it hard for you, how did you learn what you needed to know to write the book, and much more. Maintaining a website that connects you to your readers can help you develop a fan base of readers who may buy more of your books.

The website does not need to be complex, in fact, it is better to have a simple website that is easily navigated. Use a simple white background with black type. It is easier to read than any other combination of colors. Use an easy to read typeface so readers are not struggling to make out the letters.   Make the font size at least 10 points.   Slightly larger sizes, like 11 and 12 points, will make your site accessible to more people.   Always include instructions on where to purchase your book.

Put your website address on your book cover, all correspondence, and your business cards.   If you pass out bookmarks or brochures or any other marketing perks, make sure your website address is plainly displayed.

Try to include something active on your website.   If you produce a newsletter, have a sign up page.   If you like to hear from readers, provide your e-mail address.   Ask for comments from your readers about your book.   Find ways to interact with your audience.   It is rewarding for you to connect with people who enjoy the subject you write about and it reinforces the connection between yourself and the reader.

Update your website regularly.   Post new material at least monthly and invite readers to return to learn more about you and your book's topic.   Maintaining a continuing relationship with your readers is important to future business.   It also keeps you in tune with readers' interests and can lead you to more book topics or more material for your website.

Setting up Book Signings

As the publisher of your book, you will be responsible for setting up book signings.   Book signings are important additions to any author's marketing strategy.   You will meet face-to-face with readers.   You have the opportunity to establish a personal connection with your fan base. Unless you are a celebrity with a dedicated public relations specialist working with you, you will probably not have fans lined up outside the bookstore anxiously awaiting their chance to meet you. Instead, you will have to promote your book to people who have never heard of you or your book.

Your first signing is a little intimidating because you do not know what to expect. The following sections will provide ideas and knowledge about how to successfully run a book signing.

Contacting Bookstores to Set up a Signing: The first hurdle to cross is to find a bookstore willing to host a signing for you. There are literally thousands of people publishing books these days. Bookstores often get calls from publishing companies or authors requesting time for a signing. Many bookstore event managers are absolutely wonderful about supporting authors, even unknown authors. Call a bookstore you would like to have sponsor a signing and ask to speak to the person who sets up book signings. Be prepared to explain who you are and give a 20 second blurb about your book. Ask if they have any dates open for a signing. If you get negative responses, be polite and ask them to keep you on their list.

Some stores only do signings during November and December when they get the most foot traffic in their stores. Some stores never sponsor signings and some stores schedule signings throughout the year in an effort to generate traffic. You will not know a particular store's policy until you get in touch with them.

Setting up Signings at Events: You can also hold book signings at church bazaars, street fairs, craft shows, toy stores (if it is a children's book), and gift stores. For some of these events, you will pay a table fee. Check on the fees associated with any event so you can determine whether or not you will be able to make a profit. You may also be able to set up events at libraries especially if you are willing to speak about your book for free.

If you decide to do speaking events, ensure that you will be able to sell books at the event. Many organizations are willing to host authors if the author will speak for free.

School appearances are another possible venue. It helps if your book is written for children. However, if you have written a book for adults which high school students might have some interest in, you may be able to find a high school sponsor. Most author visits are coordinated through the school librarian. If school visits are part of your marketing plan, be sure to include instructions for coordinating a visit on your website.

Questions to Ask so you Know What to Expect: Coordinate your visit carefully before you appear so everything runs smoothly. You need answers to the following questions.

– When does the event begin and end?

– Where is the event located and how do you get there?

- Are there special instructions for unloading/loading?

- What is the venue providing (table, chair, poster, and advertising?)

- How much space are you allotted?

- If the event is outdoors, what weather protection is available or do you need to bring it?

- What paperwork do you need to fill out?

- What if any fees are applicable? How do the fees have to be paid and when?

- When you arrive, who will direct you to your space?

- If you are providing inventory, how does the payment process work?

- Will other authors be at the event?

- Is this signing being held as part of a larger event? If so, what is the name of the event?

- If this is a school visit, ask for the itinerary for the visit. You may end up working with the school's point of contact to establish the itinerary. School visits typically last all day and involve classroom speaking appearances, lunch with students or faculty, a courtesy visit with the principal, a book signing period, and readings from your book to students.

Advertising your Book Signing: While there may be some advertising of an event by the sponsoring agency, you will definitely want to advertise that you will be there signing books. Be prepared to devote some effort to getting the word out about your appearance.

- Send out press releases to local newspapers and websites which list community events.

- Pay for an advertisement in the local newspaper.

- If there is a local e-mail group for community events, submit the information for your event.

- Post signs around the community.

- Leave flyers at local gathering spots.

- Post the event information on your website.

- Send out an e-mail inviting your fans, friends, and family to join you there.

- Send postcards announcing your signing.

- Text, twitter, and Facebook the information for your signing.

- Leave a message on your phone's answering machine with the event details.

- Mention the event to people you meet. Let them know where to get more information and invite them to come.

- If you can get a radio or TV interview scheduled for shortly before the event, make sure you mention where your signing will be held and when.

How to Conduct a Book Signing

Book signings are often the first and only impression a reader will have of you, the author. Make it a rewarding experience for both of you. Be polite and professional. If people say they are not interested in your book, thank them, and move on to the next person. No book appeals to everybody. By the same token, do not prejudge people by their appearance as to whether or not they might be interested. Give your short cheerful greeting and let them decide if they would like to continue the conversation. The following sections give more details on how to conduct a successful signing.

What to Wear:
- As a general rule, wear business clothes. You want to appear professional and as something special in the store. Most people do not wear business clothes into the bookstore. You want to readers to be able to tell right away that something special is happening and you are part of it.
- Make sure your footgear is comfortable as you will spend a lot of time on your feet.
- Make sure your clothes are in good repair.
- Women—check to make sure there are no embarrassing gaps when you bend over to get a book. If you wear a skirt or dress, make sure it will not fly up if the weather is windy. It is a little flustering to say the least, to have your skirt floating around your head as you make your way into or out of the store!
- Dress as a character in your book if you wish, to attract attention, particularly for a children's book.

What to Bring with You:
- Bring permanent archival pens to sign the books. You can find them at art supply stores and scrapbooking sections of craft stores. Non-archival pens result in signatures which fade over time.
- Bring water in a sealable bottle. Your throat will get dry from all the talking you will do. Do not keep the bottle

on the table, put it at your feet. That way there is no chance of spilling on the books.
- Bring table display items. A table cloth, book ends or supports, bookmarks, business cards, and postcards summarizing your book including where to order it.

Book Signing Tips:
- Always be polite to everyone who stops at your table.
- Be cheerful and outgoing without being pushy.
- Have several prepared phrases to include with your autograph worked out before your signing so you do not have writer's block at the signing table.
- Greet people as they come through the door. Come up with a quick greeting that invites them to stop and talk with you. "Hello, new book by local author. Would you like to check it out?" Do not be surprised or hurt if you get a lot of "no" answers. Thank them and greet the next person through the door.
- Create energy around your signing booth with balloons, candy, a poster of you, or a colorful table cloth.
- Always double-check name spellings. There are so many unusual spellings these days and readers will appreciate having their name spelled correctly.
- Be helpful to the bookstore staff. They are supporting your efforts. They deserve your appreciation.
- Thank store personnel at the end of the signing for hosting you. Send a written note of thanks within a week of your signing.

How to Get Paid for the Books you Supply:

- Inventory your books prior to your arrival at the signing.
- Ask the bookstore person who is sponsoring your signing for a copy of any paperwork they want you to fill out.
- Check with store personnel about inventory processes for signings. Some stores have store personnel verify both the starting and ending inventories. Other stores rely on your inventories but check their sales register records at the end of the day.
- Fill out the store paperwork and request a copy for your files.
- Ask when you might expect payment (usually two weeks to a month).
- If you do not receive the payment within the estimated time, call the person who helped you set up the event and politely explain that you have not yet received payment. Ask her for help in resolving the issue.

Where to Find Other Ideas for Marketing Your Books

There are many ways to market your book. Do a search on "marketing ideas for books" and "book marketing" to find articles, books, and websites on the subject.

The following websites offer ideas which may fit your situation. We found these websites particularly helpful when we started our journey into publishing.

http://www.bookmarket.com/   John Kremer published a helpful book titled, "1001 Ways to Market Your Books". Many libraries carry this book.

http://www.amarketingexpert.com Subscribe to their free newsletter titled, "The Book Marketing Expert Newsletter".

There you are. We have demystified publishing and have shared with you lots of great information on how to get your book published. Now, do your research and then go for it! We wish you luck on your book publishing journey!

Appendix A: Glossary of Publishing Terms

-A-

Advance against Royalties—A payment to the author from the publisher based on the projected royalties the publisher expects to realize through book sales. It is only an advance. If book sales do not meet projections, the publisher is usually entitled to reclaim the royalty. Read your contract carefully.

Artistic Medium—The ink, paint, or other form of material used to create art work.

Artistic Style Elements—Color, line style, page coverage, art genre.

Aspect Ratio—The height compared to the width of a book. The aspect ratio is particularly important in choosing or creating illustrative material since it affects how such material can be laid out on a page.

-B-

Backlist—Once a book is past its new release period, the publisher will decide whether or not the book will remain in print. If the publisher decides to keep the book in print, the book will be "backlisted" or put on the publisher's "backlist". These books are no longer actively marketed but are still available for sale. If the publisher prints a catalog, the book will appear in the backlist portion of the catalog. If the publisher decides not to keep the book on its backlist, the book is remaindered.

Back matter—The material after the conclusion of the narrative text. The material selected will be based on the nature of the book, the intended page count, and the signature size. Possible back matter includes:

Index—An alphabetically organized listing of terms with page numbers denoting their occurrence throughout the book.

Notes—Explanatory notes or citing of references for material in the book which is not fully expanded in the narrative text.

Bibliography—Listing of books, articles, or websites with additional material of interest to the reader.

Glossary—Explanation of terms used in the book.

Resource Listing—A listing of sources material for crafts, gardening, food or any other activity explained in the book.

Credits—A listing of contributors for specific material included in the book, usually photographs, illustrations, graphs, and the like.

Offers by the Publisher—A page providing information on any special offers by the publisher.

Author and Illustrator Biographies—Usually short biographical notes on the author and illustrator and possibly a photograph of each is provided in the final pages of a book or on the rear book jacket.

Barcode—A series of vertical bars representing the numbers 0 through 9 read by laser scanners and used for inventory control.

Bleed—To print something so that part of it is cut off by the edge of the page. This allows the color to go to the edge of the trimmed page. Accuracy in printing and trimming is such that an area of tolerance must be factored into the design. If not factored in, the resulting document may have odd narrow strips of white at the page edges.

Book Binding—Bindings are the way the pages of a book are secured at the spine and covered front and back.

Case Bound—A hardcover book with pages glued, stitched or both at the spine.

Comb—A plastic or metal series of prongs which hold the pages together. The cover and back can be either hard or paperback. Usually used when the book's use requires it to open flat.

Perfect bound—A thick paperback cover which is glued to the pages. The cover can be printed in color and laminated.

Saddle-stitched—A book with the pages securely stitched along the spine. Most saddle-stitched books are then bound with a hardcover.

Book Category—There are numerous approaches to categorizing books including Bowkers (the providers of ISBNs), other cataloguing services (like Dustbooks for small publishing houses), and the Library of Congress. Examples of categorizations include fiction, non-fiction, biography, self-help, cooking, youth, picture books, travel, and humor.

Book Layout software—A computer software program which enables book designers to arrange all the textual and graphic material used in a book.

Quark—Quark, which is both the company name and the name of the product, sparked the desktop publishing revolution with the release in 1987 of Quark Desktop which allowed precision typography, layout, and color control capabilities for the desktop computer.

InDesign—Created by Adobe, InDesign is designed to integrate with other Adobe products like Photoshop and Illustrator for desktop publishing.

MS Publisher— Microsoft created Publisher to allow designers to meet common business printing needs. It can be used to lay out books although it does not have the sophistication of either Quark or InDesign. However, it is suitable for most book layouts and is significantly less expensive.

-C-

Coffee table—Large books of full color photographs or artwork and usually very little text.

Colophon—A publisher's emblem or trademark often used on the title page and the book spine or back cover.

Copyeditor—Corrects errors of typing, fact, and grammar; improves awkward sentences and paragraphs; applies a consistent grammatical usage to the entire work (styling); marks different parts of the text so the designer and type-setter can use the correct and consistent typefaces, font sizes, numbering, etc..

Copyright—A form of legal protection to the creator of a unique work which provides the owner the right to control how a creative work is used. Copyright is provided automatically to the author of any original work covered by the law as soon as the work is created. The author does not have to formally register the work, although registration makes it easier to pursue legal action against violators. A copyright is comprised of a number of exclusive rights, including the right to make copies, authorize others to make copies, make derivative works (serialize a work, make a movie or cartoon, audio book, etc.), sell and market the work, and perform the work. Any one of these rights can be sold separately through transfers of copyright ownership. Copyright covers unpublished as well as published works. U.S. law extends copyright protection for 50 years beyond the life of the author.

Customer—A publisher may have several different sets of customers. One set is distributors and wholesalers, another is bookstores and other retail outlets, and the final set is what is called an "end" customer—the consumer who actually reads the book.

Customer fulfillment—Order processing, shipping, invoicing, and resolution of any difficulties.

-D-

Deliverable—work to be delivered; a piece of work identified in a contract with time and content specified that is part of a larger project.

Desktop publishing software—Computer program which allows a book designer to create the book layout precisely. Printing may be done on a locally attached printer or by commercial printing companies.

-E-

E-book—A book designed to be read through an electronic device either a computer or an eBook reader.

Editor—Can refer to a text or copy editor who prepares a text for publishing or, more broadly, to the publishing supervisor who controls the overall content of a book, newspaper, or magazine.

End customer or End consumer—The person who buys the book with the intention of reading it and, perhaps, adding it to their personal library.

Endorsements—Positive statements about the book or author by authoritative sources which might include other authors, experts, or celebrities.

-F-

Font—A full set of characters of the same design (typeface) and size.

Font size—Typically refers to the distance between the top and the bottom of the highest and lowest points in the alphabet of a particular font. The unit of measure is called a point.

Front matter—Material which appears before the start of the narrative of the book. Possible front matter includes:

Praise for the book—Blurbs provided by reviewers, usually at the request of the publisher, but sometimes taken from published reviews.

Title page—A page listing only the title of the book.

Frontispiece—A drawing or other graphic which sets the mood of the book.

Half Title Page—A page listing the title, author, and publisher.

Copyright page—A page listing the title, author, copyright, and cataloguing data.

Acknowledgements page—A page used by the author to thank and acknowledge persons instrumental in the completion of the book.

Dedication page—A page dedicating the book to someone.

Listing of previous titles by the author—Any other titles which the author has had published are listed on this page.

Listing of illustrations—All illustrations appearing in the book are named and page numbers are cited on this page.

Table of contents—A listing of chapters and possibly sub-chapters to allow for easy reference by the reader.

Blank pages—usually inserted to meet signature requirements.

-G-

Ghost writer—A person who writes a work that is then published under someone else's name. A ghost writer's compensation may be a share of the author's income, a flat fee, or a combination of the two.

Gutter—The white space between the printing area and the binding on the two facing pages of a book.

-H-

Hook—A means of attracting or interesting somebody, especially a potential customer.

-I-

Illustrations—Any graphic material included in a book is an illustration. Examples include maps, drawings, photographs, charts, and graphs.

Imprint—The brand name under which a book is marketed. Publishers may use distinct imprints in order to market to different consumer segments.

ISBN—ISBN stands for International Standard Book Number and is a commercial identifier for books. The ISBN was 10 digits long until 1 January 2007 when ISBNs increased to 13 digits in length. The number uniquely identifies internationally published books and book-like products including CDs, books on tape, maps, educational films and videos, and digitized books. The number consists of 4 to 5 parts:

1. If the ISBN is 13 digits, the number has a 978 or 979 prefix EAN (European Article Number) that ensures no two starts are the same
2. Country or Language Code (0, 1 =English; 2 = French; and so on. Can be up to 5 digits)
3. Publisher (assigned by the agency)
4. Item Number
5. Check Digit (a single digit computed from other digits, if 10 it is replaced by "X")

There are many ISBN agencies worldwide; each agent has the exclusive right to assign ISBNs to publishers in their area/territory. For instance, the United States agency is Bowkers which is the only one authorized to assign ISBNs to publishers within the U.S., Virgin Islands, Puerto Rico and all of its territories. Once the agency assigns an ISBN to a publisher, then that publisher can assign the number to its publication. The publisher cannot re-assign, re-sell, transfer or split its assigned numbers with other publishers.

-L-

Layout—The design of a book page which shows the printer where text and illustrations will appear.

-M-

Margins—The blank spaces at the top, bottom, and sides of a page.

Mass market—Books intended for sale at department stores, drugstores, newsstands, and airports; usually small trim sizes and low grade paper.

-N-

New Release—Publishers have varying definitions of the

term, "New Release". The longest period for a "New Release" is one year. Many large publishers consider "New Release" to mean within the last six months and some even define it as within the last four months. The majority of marketing budgets are spent on new releases.

-P-

Pre-press processing—Printers take the computer file the publisher submits and transforms it to fit the requirements of their printing press equipment. Some printers still can process books laid out on paper which they then transform to film, but these printers are fewer in number each year.

Printer—A printer performs all the processes necessary to transform a laid-out book from a computer file to actual pages with a cover. They print the interior pages and the covers, assemble, trim, and package them for shipping.

Print-on-Demand—A printing process which allows books to be printed as needed instead of in large runs. By using Print-on-Demand you may print only one book or as many as is required to fill an order. The process allows for a much smaller initial investment in a book and less inventory storage, but results in a higher per book cost if compared to large print runs.

Proof—n. A printed copy used for checking corrections before the final printing of a text or image. v. To make a trial impression; to inspect a printed impression for errors.

Proof read—To read the proofs of a text and mark corrections to be made.

Publisher—Traditional publishers choose to invest in manuscripts which they plan to sell to the public. A publisher will work with an author to polish a manuscript, edit and design the book including obtaining illustrative material necessary for the book, arrange for printing, shipping and distribution, handle registrations, marketing, selling, and payment of royalties.

Self publishing—Self publishers must handle all of the responsibilities of the traditional publisher themselves. Certain portions of the publishing process may be outsourced to competent help.

Subsidy publisher—Subsidy publishers will publish anything which an author pays them to publish. They may provide a range of services including printing, some book design, distributing, and some assistance with marketing usually for additional fees.

Vanity publisher—Another name for subsidy publisher.

-R-

Remaindering—Books which are not selling well will be liquidated at a greatly reduced price. Although the publisher loses money, they recoup as much as possible and free inventory space for a new book which they hope will fare better in the market.

Reversion—A provision to return the rights to a work to the author if the book has been out of print for a specified period of time.

Reviews—The word, "reviews", has several meanings in the publishing world. The first is a review by a publishing house or company. This review is done by an editor to determine whether or not the manuscript fits into one of the company's publishing programs and if the company is willing to invest in the property.

Another meaning of review is a critique of a soon-to-be published or published book. These reviews are conducted by journalists and critics who write for newspapers, magazines, and journals. These reviews help market a book because many people read these reviews and subsequently buy the book. These reviews are highly valued by the publishing industry and publishers provide review copies of books to book critics regularly.

And finally, the word review can mean thoughts by the general public about the book. These usually appear on internet vending sites. These reviews have some value to a buyer who has already found the book on the vendor's site. A good review of this type may be helpful in the final sale of the book, but it does not usually have wide enough reach to help buyers find the book in the first place.

Royalties—The agreed percentage the author will make from the sale of each copy of the book. Subject to negotiation.

-S-

Signature—A grouping of pages printed simultaneously on a large sheet of paper which is then folded to produce a booklet. Multiple signatures are sewn or glued together to make up a book. Signature sizes vary according to the printing equipment. Common signature sizes are 4, 8, 16, and 32. Ask your printer what signature size he produces so you can plan your book layout properly.

Specialty books—Books intended for the bookstores, gift shops and museums, usually manufactured with novel features like pop-ups, very large or small final trim sizes, integrated book markers, and so on.

Spine—The join of the pages and the cover of a book which goes over the binding. If of sufficient width, the title of the book, the author's name and, perhaps, the colophon of the publisher may be printed on the spine.

Style sheet—A reference created for a particular publication listing the choices for typeface, grammar, layout specifications, and so on to result in internal consistency for the document. Style sheets may be used by the author, editors, typesetters, book designers, and others involved in the publication process.

Subsidiary rights—Aside from the right to publish the work in book form, many publishers also purchase the movie, audio-book, electronic, translation, first serial (excerpts printed in magazines), and other rights.

-T-

Templates—Printers provide templates showing the confining layouts of a book page depending on several factors including the page size, the binding type, and paper choice. Margins, bleed areas, layout size, and gutter allowance give book designers the constraints within which the printed material must be arranged in order to print correctly.

Trade—Refers to booksellers and those books (trade books) designed to be sold through "the trade" as opposed to books designed to be sold through specialty shops, book club programs, or other marketing channels.

Trim size—The final size of a book once the printing process is complete and the page edges have been trimmed.

Typeface—A particular style of an alphabet and accompanying characters like numbers and punctuation.

Examples include **Times New Roman**, Arial, and **Palatino Linotype**.

-U-

UPC—UPC stands for Universal Product Code and it is the twelve digit barcode. Printed on a product, it identifies that product as well as the producing company. It also allows retailers to track inventory and sales of products. General retailers use UPCs. Bookstores use ISBNs for the same function.

Appendix B: Author and Illustrator Resources

Authors—

- *Chicago Manual of Style*—Correct use of the English language
- *Writers Digest*—tips on writing and publishing
- *Literary Marketplace*™—listing of publishers, agents, and other publishing resources
- *Writer's Market*—listing of current markets for all types of writing including articles
- *Publisher's Weekly*™—current information about the book market, conventions, deals being made by mid- and large-size publishers
- Writing Clubs and classes — provide feedback on your work

Book Designers—

Book Layout Software Options:
    Quark
    InDesign
    MS Publisher
    Abode Acrobat & Distiller
    Photoshop or other graphics manipulation software

Illustrators —

- Society of Children's Book Writers & Illustrators at http:/www.scbwi.org
- *Writing with Pictures: How to Write and Illustrate Children's Books* by Uri Shulevitz

Appendix C: Book Publishing and Printing Resources

Inclusion in this list does not constitute an endorsement. Annotations in parentheses are additional information and not part of the website address.

Subsidy Publishers:

http://www.AuthorHouse.com
http://www.CreateSpace.com (Amazon.com subsidiary)
http://www.dogearpublishing.net
http://www.iUniverse.com

http://www.Lulu.com (with three special programs for publishing books by children—Books By You (ages 8 and up), Aspiring Authors (grades K-8), and Comic Book Creator.)

http://www.publishamerica.com
http://www.vantagepress.com
http://www.Xlibris.com

Search terms: publishing; self publishing

Print-on-Demand Printers:

http://publishing.booklocker.com
http://www.booksurge.com (Amazon.com subsidiary)
http://www.lightningsource.com
http://www.lulu.com

Search terms: print on demand printer, printondemand printer

Traditional Publishers:

Use **Literary Market Place**™ to get information on publishers. Library Reference sections usually have this two-volume publication.

Volume 1: publishers, literary agents, editorial services, trade associations and foundations, calendar of events, book trade courses, awards and prizes, and books and magazines for the trade.

Volume 2: public relations (including TV and radio programs for books), book reviewers, book clubs, manufacturers, prepress services, distributors and wholesalers, consultants, employment agencies, translators, artist & art services.

Also available as a searchable database for a fee at http://www.literarymarketplace.com/lmp/us/index_us.asp

Examples of the numbers of publishers for different book categories:

African American Studies, pg 373, over 210 publishers
Biography, pg 382, over 420 publishers
Children's Books, pg 336, about 490 publishers
Ethnicity, pg 397, over 140 publishers
Human Relations, pg 410, over 140 publishers
Juvenile & Young Adult Books, pg 346, about 420 publishers
Science Fiction Books, pg 435 and 436, about 140 publishers
Social Studies/Sociology, pg 437, over 280 publishers
Women's Studies, pg 443, over 280 publishers

Note 1: There are many more categories than we list here. There are also over 40,000 book publishers in the US and Canada.

Note 2: No traditional publishers show in the returns by internet search engines. This is because subsidy publishers have optimized their pages to show up for any of the standard search terms one might try to find a traditional publisher.

Publish Today!

Other Sources for Traditional Publisher contact information:
These publications can also be found in library reference sections and at bookstores. These publications are updated annually.

Writer's Market
Novel & Short Story Writer's Market
Children's Writer's & Illustrator's Market
Christian Writer's Market Guide

Offset Printers:

Submit print requirements & get quotes from printers around the world by visiting:

http://www.printindustry.com/

Most printing companies have websites and you can submit manuscripts by uploading files of the type specified by the individual printing company. The most commonly accepted file types include Quark, InDesign, and PDF. Example offset printers follow:

http://www.bookmasters.com/
http://www.ecprinting.com/pod.html
http://www.gorhamprinting.com/4information/guidelines.htm
http://www.instantpublisher.com/
http://www.tshore.com/
http://www.whitehallprinting.com/

Search terms: book printer; offset book printer

Appendix D: Trade Discounts and How They Work

A trade discount is the percentage off the retail price which provides the compensation for the distribution chain between the publisher and the end customer. The publisher sets the trade discount and lists the discount in its catalog, with Bowker's, and with any wholesaler or distributor the publisher is using to distribute the book. Here is an example of how this works using numbers which make the math easy.

An example: Book Retail Price is $20.00. The Publisher offers the book at a trade discount of 50% to the book trade.

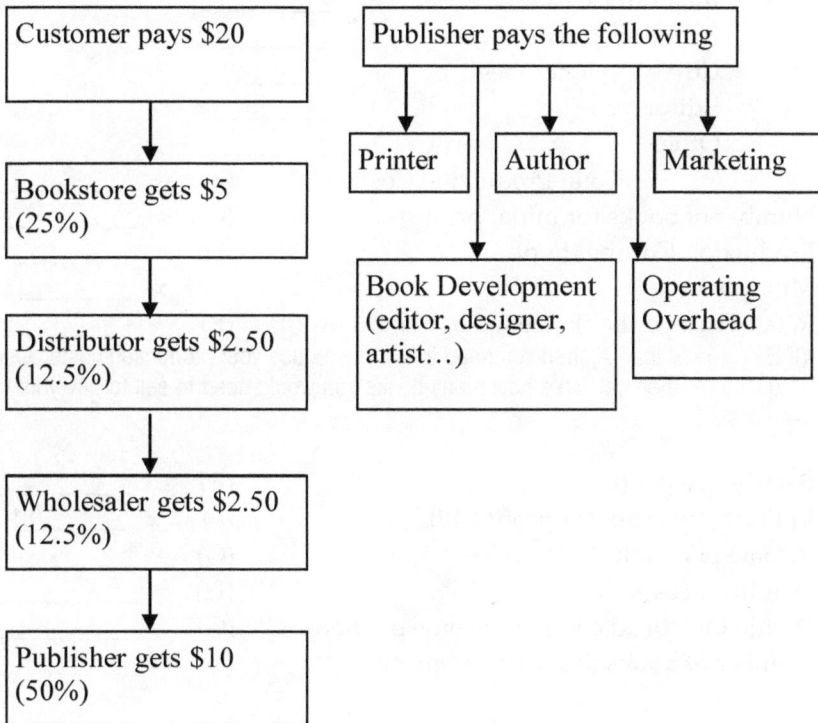

```
Customer pays $20            Publisher pays the following
       |                        |        |          |
       v                        v        v          v
Bookstore gets $5          Printer   Author   Marketing
(25%)
       |                                |        |
       v                                v        v
Distributor gets $2.50     Book Development   Operating
(12.5%)                    (editor, designer,  Overhead
       |                   artist...)
       v
Wholesaler gets $2.50
(12.5%)
       |
       v
Publisher gets $10
(50%)
```

Appendix E: Worksheet for Setting the Retail Price of Your Book

Here is a worksheet for calculating and comparing your retail price to see if the book can be profitable. You can rework your plan for production until the production costs are such that making a profit is a reasonable expectation.

Researched retail price of similar books   (A)   _____

Calculate Total Production Costs (add the following):

Rights payments		_____
Book set up fees	+	_____
Print cost of initial run	+	_____
Catalog fees	+	_____
Proof fees	+	_____
Illustrator fees	+	_____
Book Designer fees	+	_____
Cover Designer fees	+	_____
Editor fees	+	_____
Other	+	_____

Total Production Costs   (B)   =   _____
Number of books for initial print run   (C)   ÷   _____
Production Cost per book   (D)   =   _____
Multiply by   x   2.5
Retail Price per book needed to make a profit*   (E)   _____

*(If E is greater than A, then you need to work to reduce your production costs. Once E is equal to A, then calculate how many books you would need to sell to pay your overhead costs.)

Retail Price per book   (E)   _____
Multiply by expected profit (.10)   (F)   x   0.10
Income per book   (G)   =   _____
Overhead costs   (H)   _____
Divide Overhead costs by Income per book   (G)   ÷   _____
Number of books to sell before profit   (I)   _____

Meet the Authors

Celia and Mack Webb hammer away at their keyboards tucked away in the peaceful Virginia horse country. When not writing, publishing, or speaking, they pull on their Wellingtons and putter around their large organic garden.

Pilinut Press, Inc., founded in 2006, is an independent publishing company. Think of Pilinut Press when you want enjoyable reading for the whole family with an "easy-on-the-eye" style. We support our readers and educators through our Reference Desk feature on the company website which offers free lesson plans, articles, "printables", interviews, and more.

Our quality books are available through on-line book vendors like Amazon.com and your local bookstore as a special order item.

Available Titles:

Can You Keep a Secret?
ISBN: 978-0-9779576-4-4

Danny and the Detention Demons
ISBN: 978-0-9779576-2-0

Little Bianca
ISBN: 0-9779576-0-8

Seoul-Full Letters
ISBN: 978-0-9779576-6-8

The Snickerdoodle Mystery
ISBN: 978-0-9779576-5-1

Webb's Wondrous Tales Book 1
ISBN: 0-9779576-1-6

Webb's Wondrous Tales Book 2
ISBN: 978-0-9779576-3-7